Shadows

Shadows

Gene Kimmet

Illustrations by
Sarah Hasty Williams

CANOPIC
PUBLISHING

Canopic Publishing
601 Indigo Lane
Woodstock, IL 60098
www.canopicpublishing.com

Copyright © 2019 by Gene Kimmet

All rights reserved under International and Pan-American Copyright Conventions. Published in the United States by Canopic Publishing, Woodstock, Illinois.

Virginia Smith Rice, Editor

Book design by Phil Rice
Cover art and design by Sarah Hasty Williams

ISBN-13: 978-0-9997182-0-9

In memory of my wife, Gloria, with whom I shared a marriage of sixty-six years. Our mutual respect and her support of me in the shared pursuit of fine arts has been paramount in the publication of this book.

She is sadly missed.

Checkmate	13
Loss	15
Waltz	17
Uncle Jim	18
Aunt Lillian	19
Hog Creek	21
Anecdotal	23
First Snow	24
In the Presence of Violets	25
Sometimes	27
Appalachian Memories	28
Hitchhiking across the Y Bridge	29
Traveling East on Route US 20 through Iowa	30
Regrets	32
Interlude	33
Free Rider	35

II

The Hawk that Loops the Sky in Graceful Flight	39
Final Frontier	40
A Long Lost Letter from Albert to Mileva	41
Rossini Reconsiders His Final Opera	42
The Expedition Encounters a Time Warp	43
Bonaparte	45
Mickey Mouse's Version of the Big Bang	46
Chipmunk Slayer	47

III

The Old Dreamer	51
Thanksgiving	52
Taking Jenny to Port Washington	53
Shadows	54
Gathering Mushrooms in the Cemetery	56
Winters	59
The Blooming	60

Shadows

I

Checkmate

> *God moves the player,*
> *He in turn the piece*
> *But what God beyond God*
> *Starts the round of time*
> *And dust and dream*
> *And agonies.*
> — *"Chess," Jorge Luis Borges*

When my son was eight
I taught him to play chess.
Within two months, he never
Lost to me again.

At that age he had no guile
And his habit of running
Into another room to watch
Bugs Bunny on television
While I pondered my next move
Was no more than innocent
Awareness of his skill.

My own sense of lack
Was somewhat mollified
When two years later he was
Chosen to play, along with
Eight adult members
Of a chess club, against
A state champion.

He did not win but was one
Of the last three to fall.
I still remember how frail
And tired he looked when he
Came home late that night,
How hard it was for him
To fall asleep.

Now his hair is turning gray
And when we walk together
He slows that I may not be
Left behind. Each grown aware
That dreams of being kings or knights
Are often not to be.

Loss

It was as if an evil God
Had thrust a finger through a dike
Against a sea of memories

That slowly drained for seven years
Till every image was erased
And only blackness filled the void.

Her children's names and faces gone,
Six decades with her husband gone,
All the summer days forgotten.

And even how to say a word,
How to swallow, how to breathe,
Until a kinder kind of death.

How can I now remember her?
Running down a hill at seven
Her blond hair streaming out behind,

Her wedding day, her first born child?
There is no way to draw a line
Through that dark slide into emptiness.

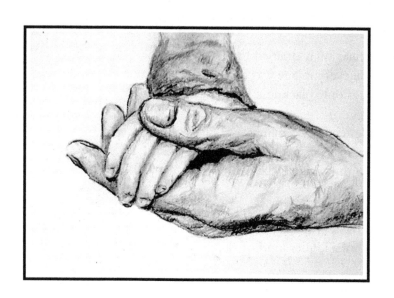

Waltz

In a small town square with piped
Music, a burly man with blue eyes
And blond beard streaked with gray

Reaches one long finger down
To the grasp of a tiny child
With almond Asian eyes,

Leads her up the wooden steps
To the gazebo's concrete floor,
Bows, sweeps her into his arms,

Whirls with perfect time
To the flow of a waltz that fills
The empty park, while she

With glowing eyes and shy smile
Floats far above the floor.
Suddenly this man who has

A look of beer and Harleys
Becomes a prince in glittering hall,
And in this scene where such disparate

Partners turn with easy grace
I cannot but think that Strauss
Might somewhere watch with wonder

Pleased to find in a world
Of doubt and anger, this glimpse
Of something right.

Uncle Jim

Raw-boned with awkward gait,
He lived in a small trailer
On the banks of a muddy river
That wound its way across
The flat fields of northern Ohio
To its rest in a dirty lake.

He wore old black pants, scuffed shoes,
Suspenders, spit tobacco juice
Through a picket of yellow teeth,
Lived mostly on beer and hot dogs,
Spent his final years fishing
For carp in the slow current.

He was already getting old
When I was a boy. Now I am old,
And what I remember most
Of him is the way he and his hat
Descended together into ruin.

When I was young, the sweat band
Was marked with a pattern faintly
Resembling a crude map.
As decades passed, the stain
Spread and in his later years,
Engulfed the hat.

When he lay hatless in his
Final rest, there were no tears,
No words of praise. We ate
The plain and silent supper,
Drove home to our separate lives –

No one mentioned the hat.

Aunt Lillian

With nowhere else to go
She shared a tiny house
With the boy, his three sisters
And parents. She rose at five
Each morning, walked in winter dark
To a kitchen job, guided
Along shattered sidewalks
By the dim beam of a flashlight.

Past hunched figures of men
On their way to the mills, past
The fierce German shepherd
Straining at his chain, through
Coal smoke that sprinkled soot
On snow, through the dim flicker
Of refinery flares, the acrid
Taste of iron from red smoke
Of the furnaces, and always
Accompanied by the shrill call
Of steam whistles on trains.

She had a son, born one month
Before the boy. He died within
A month. In her emptiness
She turned to the boy, showered him
With love in a scarce time.
When he grew older and roamed
The streets with ragged friends
She would call to him across
The square, "Genie Boy, Genie Boy,
Come with me, I'll buy you coffee,
Ice cream." He always went
While the others chided him in glee.

Now at the end
Of his own seasons, breathing
Clean air under a clear sky,
He wonders if, by some
Unlikely miracle, a spirit
One month his elder
Sits with her in a kinder place.

Eating ice cream, drinking
Black coffee from those thick
White mugs, far from the smoke
Of mills, rumble of freights,
The confinement of existing
In a single room, the fear
Of dying alone.

Hog Creek

Toward evening
In late summer, the boy
Walks a worn path that follows
The river bank. He carries
A twenty-two rifle, passes
Tattered houses, switch yards,
Smoking mills. He is on his way
To the dam at the edge of town
Where a giant Cottonwood
Leans over the dirty river.

He comes here to escape the anger
That inhabits his house, despair
That lurks in its darkest corners.
Crouching behind a spillway buttress
He waits for the flocks of blackbirds
That roost at night in the towering tree.
They come in groups of tens or twenties,
Chattering like small school children.

Steadying the gun on a concrete edge
He aims, squeezes the trigger.
A bird drops into the river, the rest
Fly away. As light fades they come
In larger flocks, some remain
After the first shot. In ones and twos
He culls them from the tree.

Finally, out of shells, he climbs
To the concrete top, watches
A ragged line of small dark forms
Drifting on the brown current
That bends out of sight
Into the deep woods.

He turns to watch the sunset,
Comforted by the mauve
And rose and ochre patterns
In the clear sky, upwind from
The mills, away from the town.

Savoring the peaceful slice of time,
He waits until the last color fades,
Then pockets the bolt from the gun,
Slowly retraces the path leading
Back toward home and darkness.

Anecdotal

Sam Gowdy, a short round man
With a shock of white hair
And a burr in his voice,
Convinced us that he,
As a young man in Scotland,
Was a world champion wrist breaker.

We had never heard of such a sport
And later when I sought to verify,
I was, of course, denied. Yet through
Those early years we marveled
At his great gnarled hands, reveled
In his company.

In that grim place
Where mills roared night and day,
Flags of red smoke trailed from stacks,
Sprinkled soot on window sills
And stained the sky, we did not seek
For truth, we searched for heroes.

First Snow

On a late November night
The boy would walk in wonder
To watch the town transform.

Dirty roofs, gravel drives
Fading to white silence, weeds
In vacant lots woven into lace.

The harsh refinery flares
Dimmed to a peach glow, black
Shadows of shops drawing on

Pale coats. Even the call
Of trains muted in damp air.
Hour after hour he roamed

The sidewalk limits, past rows
Of darkened houses where men
Slept the sleep of heavy toil.

He reveled in the interlude
When everything was new,
His solitary footprints wandering

The corners of a kingdom
Before sun and soot
Claimed the dream.

In the Presence of Violets

Mid-April and the boy
Follows the river, past stacks
Trailing flags of red smoke
From the open hearth furnaces,
Past refinery flares that cast
An orange glow on rows
Of run-down houses.

Past the dam at the edge of town
Where an undulating raft of carp,
Killed by the water's toxic stew,
Piles against the dam.

Fifteen and alone, he heads
Toward a copse of trees
Where the spring before, he found
Small patches of violets
In a rare strip of dark soil
On a clay bank.

This year they are legion.
A haze of blue on a field of green,
Frail stems quiver in breeze,
A miracle of color bursting
Into a dull landscape.

He sits for an hour
On an island of peace
Until a gray curtain of rain
Draws across the bright scene,
Then rises, turns toward home.

At supper in the grim kitchen
A sister asks him why he's wet.
The silent father, weary
From the long day in the mill
Does not look up. The boy shrugs,
Files the memory away.

Sometimes

In the smoke shadow of mills,
In the dark days that crept
Like a current under a river
Of clouds, we were struck by
A shaft of sunlight,

The sound of father laughing,
Mother singing in the kitchen,
As if a field of flowers burst
Into bloom on a winter day.

Wise in the way how quick
The light went out, how long
The pall persisted, we clung
To those magic moments.

Appalachian Memories

Hairpin turns in old cars
With bad brakes, the reek
Of whiskey. Tacky towns
With tilted streets, young girls
Giggling on corners, sullen boys
That spit as I walk by.

Dark climbing out of hollows,
Sleepless nights in railroad towns,
Bare floors in cheap hotels, all night
Rumble of trains, the lonely shrill
Of steam echoing across ridges
That hemmed the narrow valleys.

At twenty it was all adventure.
Now time has worn away that high
That hones the edge of danger.
Fear, patient in the shadows,
Creeps in to take its turn,
Like a dark mold spreading
Across a bright canvas.

Hitchhiking across the Y Bridge

"I've lived here all my life,
This is the only Y bridge
In the country. You can drive
Onto one end and get off
At the other end, or
The other end." He laughs,
Slows to a crawl to show me
The intersection in the middle
Of the Muskingum River
In Zanesville, Ohio.

A following truck rear-ends us.
The policeman who comes
Tells me to get lost. I walk away
Across the end that continues
East on U.S. Route Forty.
I am stiff and sore the next day
And forever wondering
If the old man was O.K.

Gene Kimmet

Traveling East on Route US 20 through Iowa

*In memory of Baheej Khleif, who
always chided me for not turning up
the tone at the end of my poems.*

From high ground, corn stretches
To the horizon on both sides
Of the road, a savage tail wind
Sweeps anything not tied down
Straight east.

Small towns are dwarfed
By giant elevators lined
Along shining railroad tracks.
The houses plain and white,
Pickups parked on streets,
No people anywhere in sight.

Passing through an empty town,
I pick up speed, spot something
Rolling in the road ahead –
A white sombrero.

I slow, clock its speed at forty-five,
Swing left and pass, wondering
Of the vaquero missing
Under his own hat,

Shadows

Perhaps wandering aimless
In an endless maze of corn,
Dismounted, hatless
In a howling wind, flailed
By sharp green leaves

While his hat, pristine, focused
On its own journey, heads east
At a steady clip toward
The wind shelter of the Mississippi
And the prospect of stopping
To find a home on a new head.

Regrets

They visit me on autumn days
In solitary walks in woods
Where cold rain cloaks the barren trees
And pale light shines on naked branch.

Or in the sleepless dark of night
When anxious dreams disturb my rest
And errant deeds repeat themselves,
Deeds gone awry and deeds undone.

And I, with slowing step, grown old
In winter's realm, no longer seek
For ways to turn aside the path
I've trod through my allotted time.

No longer try to justify
Or ask some power to forgive,
Aware that wisdom too late gained
Will never change what cannot change.

Interlude

Elegant in coat and tie,
He sits on a bench. A crest
Of white hair gleams, shoes polished,
A walking stick carved in ebony.
Rising, he smiles, holds out his hand.

"How good it is to see you George,
I knew it was you by the way
You threw the stick and struck
The center of that hickory trunk."

George is not my name. Could he
Have been a ragged member
Of that band of boys I knew
Who scourged this park with sticks
And stones and shouts so long ago?

The odds are small, too many years.
I look into his eyes, they are wide
With wonder, a blue so pale
They almost shade to white.
"What is your name?" I ask.
"I am George." He answers.
Wary now yet drawn, I step
Into a quiet space washed clean
Of jagged episodes.

His parted string of memories
Unveils a world of simple truths.
We share an interlude of peace
In soft September sun.

Children once again, we drift
In timeless afternoon, watching
The opiate flight of bees, tumble
Of a leaf along a path, journey
Of an ant returning home.

A chill wind draws a cloud
Across the sun. We rise, I turn
Back to a darker path, he smiles,
Resumes his walk in sunlight.

Free Rider

On the last train
From Chicago to Harvard
I share a car with three riders:
A fierce looking man drinking
Out of a flask, a teenager
With a skate board, and an old woman
Fast asleep.

It is almost eleven. There are
Only two stops left, mine is next.
As I stand in the exit, something
Seems to slide across my eyes,
Like a floater or a mote of dust.
I wipe them, whatever it is
Returns, sliding the other way.

I put my glasses on.
It is a tiny spider, suspended
On a single strand, reflected
In the dim light overhead.
I wonder how it can be fixed
To the smooth steel panel above?

It is November, thirty degrees,
How has this speck of life wandered
Into this metal desert speeding west
At eighty miles an hour toward
A cold and empty siding
At track's end?

It cannot last the night without heat
Yet, unaware and unobserved, except
By me, continues at its task as if
Its own allotted span of time
Will never end.

I have convinced myself this chosen
Set of rails will lead me to a warm
Familiar bed to rise again tomorrow
And do the things I always do.

As if the vagaries of chance control
A spider's fate yet somehow spares
The happenstance of human sentience
From an older truth – the random cast
Of dice.

II

The Hawk that Loops the Sky in Graceful Flight

The hawk that loops the sky in graceful flight
With mortal talons clasps the trembling hare
No malice hides within the hunter's might

A shadow crosses snow in bright sunlight
Reveals the raptor soaring high in air
The hawk that loops the sky in graceful flight

We seek the sun deny the coming night
The other seeker settles in his lair
No malice hides within the hunter's might

The fleeing prey cannot outrun his sight
A skill omnipotent that none can dare
The hawk that loops the sky in graceful flight

Our slowing step observed from towered height
The chase complete the circle closed with care
No malice hides within the hunter's might

Once more the game repeats the ancient rite.
With timeless patience sets again the snare
The hawk that loops the sky in graceful flight
No malice hides within the hunter's might

Final Frontier

In the year two thousand
And seventy five, when
The first men trudge

Through the fine red dust
On the arid plains of Mars,
They find a small dome

Cast of exotic metal.
Inside, seated at a table,
The perfectly preserved

And formally attired bodies
Of Amelia Earhart
And Jimmy Hoffa.

A Long Lost Letter from Albert to Mileva (August, 1905)

My Dear Mileva,

How can I ask forgiveness
For my want of wisdom?
All those arguments we had
Of gravity and space and time.
How could I know that you
Would ever grasp the abstract
Thought that ties together energy,
The speed of light, and mass?

Since we've parted, I've pondered
Many evenings on the theories
You proposed and must admit,
All the things you postulated
Are true. E really does equal
MC squared.

Remembering you always, Al

Rossini Reconsiders His Final Opera

In a parallel universe
Six-hundred years ago
A father places an apple
On the head of a frightened boy.
"You must not move," he tells him.

The peasants, gathered in the square
To watch this strange event, wonder
At this man who, rather than bow
To a tyrant's hat, would test his skill
And risk the life of his only son.

In that universe, however,
Something goes awry. Rossini
Will not celebrate the feat,
The Lone Ranger and Tonto
Will not ride the west
To the famous theme.

Nothing in their history will note
The second arrow falling from
The archer's coat as he races
Toward the stricken son, no mention
Of the apple falling unscathed
To the ground.

In that universe, as the father
Draws the bow, the boy recalls
His mother's scold,

"Walter, stop slouching
And stand up straight."

The Expedition Encounters a Time Warp

After leaving their canoes
At the source of the Missouri
And starting the terrible trek
Over the Bitter Root Mountains,
Wading in snow four feet deep,
Eating dogs and horses, the party
Unexpectedly stumbles into
A Starbucks.

Meriwether Lewis, always amenable
To new situations, is unperturbed,
"Twenty-four tall lattes for here,"
He tells the astonished girl.
The men, not having their leader's
Knack for handling shifts in time,
Stare open mouthed at the clean tables
And chairs, polished floors.

Sipping the lattes in the sudden
Warmth, some of them doze off
In their chairs. Some shed their coats
And hats, stretch out on the floor.
As the stink of wet fur and unwashed
Bodies replaces the scent of roasted
Colombian, the other customers
Scramble for the door.

Clark, fearing this is a trick
Played on them by the Blackfoot,
Orders the men back into the snow
After making sure that each man stuffs
Handfuls of those little brown napkins
Into their packs for more mundane use
As they continue on their quest for
The headwaters of the Columbia.

Gene Kimmet

Later that night, while Clark
And the other men babble
Over the day's events, Meriwether,
Working on his journal for Jefferson,
Ponders a while, decides that
some things are better unreported.

Bonaparte

A small man with towering
Ego, "The job of a woman"
He said, "Is to obey her husband."
His love of "La Belle France"
Beyond question. The Duke
Of Wellington considered
His presence on the field,
"Equal to forty-thousand men."

We view his diminutive form
Mounted on a great white horse,
Or standing in a drawing room,
One hand in his tunic, dark bangs
Gracing a smooth forehead,

His gaze surmounting the vision
Of that impossible march through
A Russian winter, soldiers stacked
Like frozen cords of wood
Along the endless roads—
"The death of a million men
means nothing to me."

His exile quarters on St. Helena
A curiosity for the rare visitor.
Courvoisier, his favorite cognac,
Still commands a higher price.
But it was his last battle
Fought in a rain soaked field
In Belgium on a single Sunday
That etches him into history;
A symbol for all defeats.

Mickey Mouse's Version of the Big Bang

The sorcerer waved a wand
Expecting a rabbit in a hat,
A bright bouquet of flowers,
A dove within a fold of silk,
Only to bring forth in a blaze
Of light the substance to form
A universe, wind the clock
Of time, fill a sea of space.

A gesture gone awry that
Freed a billion galaxies
Coiled within a single point
To start the march of slugs
And apes and kings and fools.

He could never rectify the deed,
And all the delving into space,
Prying into particles a waste,
Given the odds of finding
An apprentice with
Broom enough to
Sweep up all
Those stars
And put
Them
Back
.

Chipmunk Slayer

with apologies to James Fenimore Cooper

He is old, retired,
Out of meaningful tasks,
His attention turned to these
Small rodents who chew their way
Into his garage, build tunnels
That let water into his basement.

His weapon, an air rifle.
Unlike Cooper's hero,
He doesn't eat what he shoots,
Nor confront a landscape
Of pathless forests, armed savages.
His motto is not, "One shot, one kill."

Sometimes he stands in stocking feet
On white carpet, fires through
An open crank-out window,
Often misses. If he shoots straight,
He puts on shoes, retrieves the prize,
Drops it head first into a paper sack
That formerly carried wine.

If it's past nine AM, he puts it
In the garage until early next morning
When the park is empty, lifts it
Out by the tail, swings it into
A wooded glacial ravine, folds
The empty sack, places it
In the green barrel marked
PAPER ONLY.

Since it is biodegradable
And not thrown into the park itself,
He is comfortable with this procedure.
He drives home, makes a pot of coffee,
Carries two cups upstairs, wakes
His sleeping wife. They plan their day.

III

The Old Dreamer

No longer dreams of glass-winged dragonflies
That hawked mosquitos from the summer stream
When he was ten and walked in April's sun,
No longer dreams the chill of autumn wind
That rustled through November's dry corn stalks,
The frantic beat of wings, the shotgun's jolt
When he was seventeen and stalked the fields
To strike the pheasants from a cobalt sky.

Grown anxious now, he dreams of dingy streets,
Walks once again among the pale-faced men
Who fired the roaring furnaces at night
And slept the sun away, now wanders through
The rusted bones of mills to find the bar
And find his father's ghost still dealing cards,
Still pocketing the change the boy would glean
From the tattered chair where the old man slept.

Thanksgiving

A fly on the cold side
Of a window views,
Through multi-facet eyes,
A host of turkeys.

On the warm side
An old man surrounded
By family gazes out
At the first few flakes,

Remembers the smell
Of winter fields, the crunch
Of snow, the bright flare
Of a pheasant rising.

The fly, unable to solve
The clear barrier, and the man
Trapped in reverie, sit motionless.
Neither eats anything at all.

Taking Jenny to Port Washington

The April smelt run
Is almost finished. Dead fish
Float by the hundreds, the few
Still alive wallow erratic
On their sides, stench is heavy
In the damp air.

Our quiet procession moves
Along a breakwater that guards
The harbor from open lake.
We have brought her to this place
She loved. I have been handed a poem
To read, it is saccharine, over-written.
I am pleased she cannot hear.

Her young husband clasps the box
So tight his knuckles whiten as he
Sifts her ashes into the water.
Minnows dart at smaller bits
As they drift to the sandy floor,
Overhead the raucous cry of gulls.

Winter repeats
Its annual death, ice melts
Into spring. I search for solace
In the ordered way each thing
Returns to its destined level.

Shadows

We walk together on this late
December afternoon as we have walked
For more than half a century.

If we stand each year in sunshine
In this short season, our shadows
Never show our change.

Tall silhouettes aimed north
Across a field of snow,
Constants in a shifting world.

Steps slow, we tire, hope
Dulled by gathering years, yet
When we pause in winter sun

Our images escape
The weight of flesh,
Never age or waver.

Gathering Mushrooms in the Cemetery

Each autumn they appear,
Scattered among the rows of stones.
I find comfort in their pale forms,
Their scent of earth, touch of skin.

Selecting only the youngest,
I slice and mix with cubed
Potatoes, simmer in sweet cream.
Each bowl sprung from mortal ground,
Each ladled spoon a resurrection.

An Old Man Seeks Peace in a Winter Woods

The pour of clouds leaches color
From fading light, a lone crow
Calls from a pitching branch.

He recalls at seventeen
The spasms of a rabbit tumbled
By a twelve gauge onto a thin

Cover of snow, the flutter
Of a moth's wings captured
In a sparrow's beak,

The quiver of his father's hands
Against the pale sheets in his last bed.
Today no solace graces him
In this dark place.

The Rift

It is as if they somehow drifted
From the evenings always shared,

The wine, the candles, tones of Bach,
Touch of hands across the table,

Memories of mountains hiked,
Of summer days in silent woods.

As if a force transported them
To an empty desert island,

Two chairs faced across bare sand,
Each backing toward an endless sea.

Outstretched hands no longer touch,
Their figures dwindling, voices stilled,

Nothing left but blue of sea and sky –
The senseless slap of waves.

Winters

> *O, wind, if winter comes, can spring be far behind?*
> – Percy Bysshe Shelley

This winter wind that carries me
Through all the seasons into age
Can bring no spring, no grass turned green.

No birdsong in a waking woods,
No purple blush of violets
Or meadow scent in April breeze.

In silent darkness absolute,
Can such a thing as peace exist
In such a place?

The Blooming

"Your Hibiscus is beautiful,"
He says. She smiles, unaware
That he does not know the name
Of any other flower in her garden.
He's been walking past her house
Every morning for the last several weeks.

Today she notices his new blue shirt
And matching tie. She is wearing
New green garden shoes and a hat
With flowers on the brim to keep
The wind from her wild white hair.

Neither has spoken before. He views
The array of unknown shapes and colors,
Then nods and continues down the street,
Looking back from the corner
To see her still standing there.

Over the next days, he pores through books
With pictures and descriptions of flowers.
Mid-morning each day she watches
For his figure, the slight limp
In his long step.

In a week or so he has memorized
Several dozen plants. The last three
Were easy: Buddleia, Lantana,
Ageratum. Spoken aloud they flow
Like Shakespeare's iambic pentameter.

Shadows

On a day that hints of fall, she invites him
To dinner the following evening.
Each skips the next morning's chat, he
To get a haircut, she to unwrap
The silver and antique dishes
Stored away after her husband died.

In late afternoon, she sets the table,
Places cut flowers in a crystal vase.
The scent of roast and baked bread
Seeps through the house. He rummages
Through boxes yet unpacked from moving,
Looking for his mother's locket
Willed him long ago.

As he walks toward her house,
Gift in pocket, he grows anxious,
Like a schoolboy on a first date.
By now she has opened the wine
And turned on a recording
Of Rafe Von Williams'
"The Lark Ascending."

Her smile grows to a wide grin
As he comes up the walk,
The tiny blue tag still attached
To the sleeve of his new jacket
Like a Bachelor Button
Dancing on a string.

About the Author

Gene Kimmet is a retired professor of economics from Harper College in Palatine, Illinois.

He was born in Lima, Ohio, a town with a long history of heavy industrial production. Kimmet worked at a variety of jobs there, including lens grinder, foundry worker, service station operator, and salesman, before receiving a BA in economics from Ohio Northern University. He later earned an MA in economics from Case Western Reserve University and a post-master's degree in economics from Northern Illinois University. Kimmet has also done extensive graduate work in English and creative writing at Northern Illinois University and the University of Virginia.

Previous collections include *Recollections of My Father* (Canopic 2015), *Skipping Stone* (Dream Stone Press 2000) and *In Fee Simple* (Stormline Press 1986.)

Made in the USA
Middletown, DE
03 April 2023

27568204R00036